Who Pooped in the Park?™

Written by Gary D. Robson
Illustrated by Robert Rath

FARCOUNTRY
PRESS

To my brother, Keith.
- Gary

For Lucy and Thomas, my poop experts.
- Robert

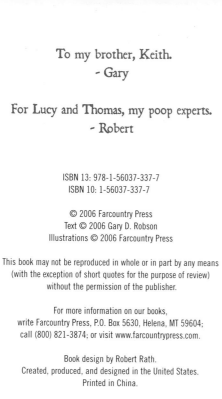

ISBN 13: 978-1-56037-337-7
ISBN 10: 1-56037-337-7

© 2006 Farcountry Press
Text © 2006 Gary D. Robson
Illustrations © 2006 Farcountry Press

For more information on our books,
write Farcountry Press, P.O. Box 5630, Helena, MT 59604;
call (800) 821-3874; or visit www.farcountrypress.com.

Book design by Robert Rath.
Created, produced, and designed in the United States.
Printed in China.

11 10 09 08 07 06   1 2 3 4 5 6

Library of Congress Cataloging-in-Publication Data

Robson, Gary D.
    Who pooped in the park?. Olympic National Park / [Gary D. Robson, Robert Rath].
      p. cm.
    ISBN-13: 978-1-56037-337-7
    1. Animal tracks--Maine--Olympic National Park--Juvenile literature. I. Rath, Robert. II. Title.
    QL768.R613 2006
    591.9741'45--dc22

                    2005016252

ENTERING
OLYMPIC
NATIONAL
PARK

"Dad? I have to go to the bathroom."
Michael squirmed in the back seat.

"We'll be at our campground in
just fifteen minutes," said Dad.
"We're in Olympic National
Park now."

"He's just nervous," said Michael's sister. "He thinks a bear's gonna eat him." She growled at Michael and made her fingers look like claws.

"Stop it, Emily," said Mom. "Nobody is getting eaten by anything."

Michael was very excited about the trip,
but Emily was right. He *was* nervous.

He had just read a book about grizzly bears.
He knew how big they could get.

And he was afraid that a hungry bear would eat
just about anything—maybe even a boy.

"I *am* kind of scared of grizzly bears," admitted Michael.

"Don't worry," Dad told him. "There are no grizzlies around here. Just black bears."

Mom reached back and held Michael's hand. She said, "We'll show you how to count a black bear's toes and never get close enough to be scared."

"Here's our campsite. Let's set up the tent. Then we can go for a walk and we'll show you what we mean," Dad said.

Michael was pretty worried about bear toes, but tried not to show it.

"Let's hurry!" said Emily. "I want to see some animals!"

Once the tent was up, the whole family went for a hike.

Emily started to complain before they even left the campground. "I haven't seen any animals yet. Maybe there aren't any here!"

"Sure there are," said Dad. "Let's see what we can learn about them from their *sign*."

"Sign?" said Michael. "You mean like a sign at the zoo?"

"In this case," replied Dad, "a sign is a clue that an animal has left behind. See the chewed-up pine cones at the base of that tree? That's a sign of a squirrel having its lunch."

"Here are some footprints," said Michael.

"Good! Tracks are animal sign, too," said Dad.

"And there's the squirrel," laughed Mom, as a Douglas squirrel ran up a tree and scolded them loudly.

the STRAIGHT
POOP
Douglas squirrels are also called chickarees or pine squirrels.

"Look, kids. Here's some squirrel scat," said Dad.

"*Scat?*" asked Emily, looking a little less grumpy. "What's *scat?*"

"It's the word hikers and trackers use for animal poop," Dad replied.

"See, Michael," said Dad. "We don't have to get up close to an animal to learn about it. Instead of a close encounter of the *scary* kind, we'll have a close encounter of the *poopy* kind."

Everybody laughed, and Mom made a gross-out face.

13

"Dad! Mom! Look over here! I found more scat!" yelled Michael. "It's a lot bigger than the squirrel scat."

"It looks like it's from a deer or an elk," said Mom.

14

ROOSEVELT ELK

BLACK-TAILED
MULE DEER

"How can you tell the difference?"
Emily wanted to know.

"The only deer around here is the
black-tailed mule deer," Dad
answered, "and it's a lot smaller
than an elk. Its scat is smaller, too.
Let's look for some more clues."

"Are these deer tracks?" Emily asked. She was starting to get interested.

"Yes!" said Mom. "They're from a mule deer. See how they're split? Deer have hooves with two parts."

the STRAIGHT POOP

Elk tracks are bigger and more rounded at the tip than deer tracks, which are pointy.

ELK

DEER

"Oh, no!" said Michael. "Here's one of its antlers. Did a bear eat the deer?" Michael looked around nervously.

Dad bent down by the antler. "No, the deer is fine. This is called a "shed" antler. The antlers fall off every winter, and the deer grows a new, bigger set the next year."

the STRAIGHT
POOP

Female deer, elk, and moose don't grow antlers. Caribou are the only members of the deer family in which both males and females have antlers.

Mom studied the ground. "This deer was in a hurry, though," she said.

Michael and Emily went over to look.

"How can you tell?" said Emily.

"The hoofprints get very far apart here," Mom explained, "and the back prints are in front of the front prints."

"It was walking backwards?" said Emily.

Mom replied, "Oh no, the deer was galloping. Something scared it, and it was moving fast."

BACK HOOVES

FRONT HOOVES

FRONT HOOVES

BACK HOOVES

WALKING   GALLOPING   PRONKING

the STRAIGHT POOP

Sometimes mule deer bounce along with all four feet hitting the ground together. This is called "stotting" or "pronking."

GALLOPING

"Here's what scared the deer," Dad said.
"There are coyote tracks and scat all around here."

"Some of the tracks are small, like they're from pups," said Mom.
"I'll bet their den is nearby."

the STRAIGHT POOP

Coyotes eat just about anything they can catch, and steal leftovers from other predators, too.

"They look like dog tracks," said Michael.

"That's because the coyote is a member of the dog family," explained Dad.

the STRAIGHT POOP

One way to tell coyote scat from dog scat is by the hair and bits of bones in the coyote scat.

COYOTE
TRACKS

BOBCAT
TRACKS

MOUNTAIN
LION
TRACKS

"Is this another coyote track?" asked Emily. "It's a lot bigger."

"It also doesn't show any claw marks," said Mom, "and the front of the big pad looks dented in. It looks more like a cat track."

Dad added, "And since it's too big to be a bobcat track, it must be from a mountain lion."

the STRAIGHT POOP

Cats can retract their claws, so their tracks don't show claw marks. Dogs can't retract their claws, so their tracks do show claw marks.

23

MOUNTAIN LION

BOBCAT

"Are they as big as panthers?" Michael asked, wide-eyed.

"Mountain lions *are* panthers," Mom said with a smile. "And they're also called cougars, painters, pumas, and catamounts. They have lots of names."

Emily spotted a pile of scat on the trail and said, "I know what this is! It's horse poop."

"Right," said Mom. "And here are some hoofprints from the horse, too."

"Those are funny-looking hoofprints," said Michael.

the STRAIGHT POOP

Horses can walk and poop at the same time, but they have to stop and stand still to pee.

"Horses don't have split hooves like deer and elk," said Dad. "It's just one part."

"I think he's talking about the horseshoes," said Mom. "They make the hoofprints look different."

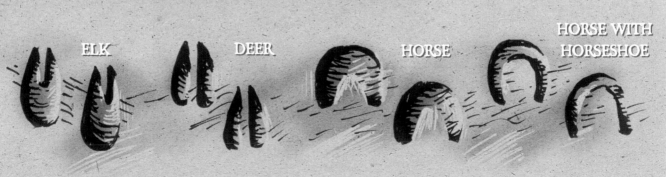

ELK   DEER   HORSE   HORSE WITH HORSESHOE

Michael looked up. "What are these white streaks on the rocks over here?" he asked.

"That's called guano," said Dad.

the STRAIGHT POOP

Bat guano makes very good fertilizer. People buy bags of it to spread in their gardens to keep their plants healthy.

"I know what that is!" exclaimed Emily. "We learned about it in school. Guano is bat poop!"

"Right," said Mom. "There are a lot of different bats in Olympic National Park. One of the most common is the little brown bat."

"Do they suck blood like vampires?" said Michael with a shudder.

"Oh no, they're just tiny bats that eat insects," said Mom with a smile. "There are no vampire bats around here."

the STRAIGHT POOP

Bats sleep hanging upside-down and like to perch in caves, trees, and holes in the rock.

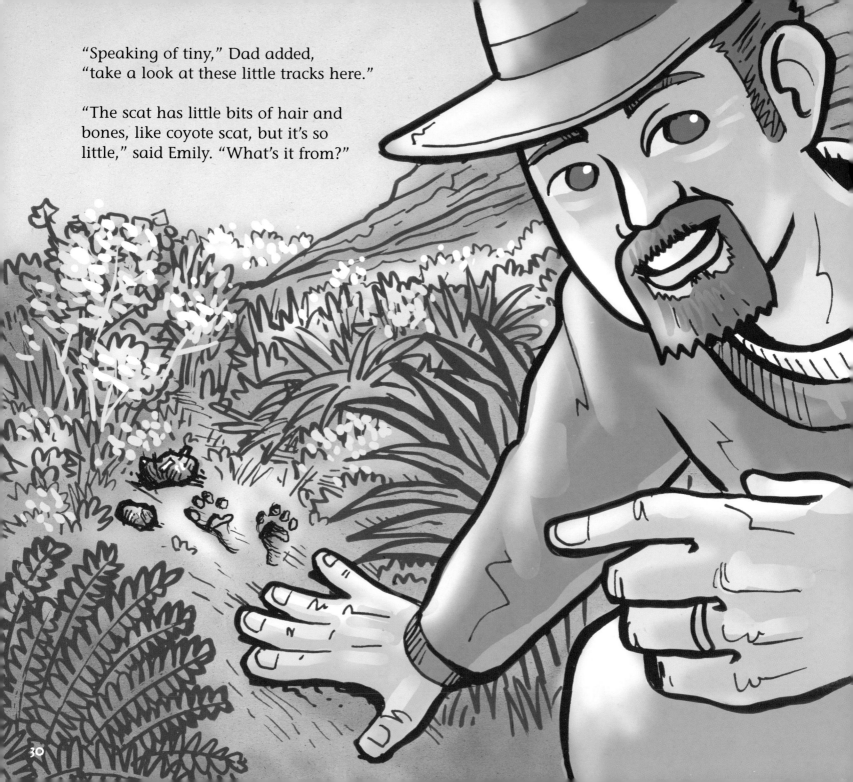

"Speaking of tiny," Dad added, "take a look at these little tracks here."

"The scat has little bits of hair and bones, like coyote scat, but it's so little," said Emily. "What's it from?"

30

Dad replied, "It's from a weasel."

"Weasels aren't much bigger than a hotdog," Mom added, "but they're very good predators. They eat mice and other small animals."

The STRAIGHT POOP

Short-tailed weasels are also called ermines, and the ones living in Canada, Alaska, and some parts of the lower 48 states usually turn white in the winter. The Olympic short-tailed weasels found in the park don't change color.

Emily looked down at the beach below. "Are those weasels in the water down there?" she asked.

"Those are sea otters. They are cousins to the weasel, but much bigger," Mom answered.

the STRAIGHT POOP

Otters are born in the water, and they spend most of their lives floating and diving. They even eat and sleep in the water.

"Look out farther," said Dad. "There's a gray whale spouting. It probably just surfaced after a long dive."

the STRAIGHT
POOP

Gray whales pass by Olympic National Park in the spring and fall on their long yearly swims between Alaska and Mexico. A few spend the summer here and are seen quite often by visitors who hike along the coast.

33

Emily noticed something strange on the tree. "Is this more bat poop?" she asked.

"That poop is from an owl," Dad said. He looked down at the ground below the tree and added, "See these tracks with two toes pointing forward and two pointing backward, and the owl pellets around the base of the tree?"

"Owl pellets?" said Emily.

"Owls eat their prey whole," explained Dad. "The parts they can't digest, like hair and bones, get coughed up in a pellet like this."

the STRAIGHT POOP

Studying owl pellets is a great way to find out what owls eat. They dine on small animals such as mice, birds, and lizards.

"Yuck!" said the kids.

"I think this is from a spotted owl," said Mom.

"There aren't very many places you can find spotted owls anymore," said Dad. "Olympic National Park still has the old-growth forests they live in, though."

the STRAIGHT POOP

Owls see very well at night, but they aren't blind during the day, as some people believe.

"Here's another track," Michael called out. "It has five toes like a weasel track, but it's a lot bigger."

"It's a raccoon track," Mom told him.

"We have raccoons back home, don't we?" asked Michael.

"Raccoons live almost everywhere in the United States," answered Mom. "They can swim and climb trees, and they eat all kinds of food, including fruit, nuts, insects, eggs, and small animals."

the STRAIGHT POOP

Raccoons are very clever and skilled. They can work doorknobs and take the lids off of garbage cans.

Because raccoons can get into backpacks, coolers, and food bags, campers should use special animal-resistant food containers.

Suddenly Michael exclaimed, "Wow! What happened to this tree?"

"Something was sharpening its claws, Michael, and if you look how high those scratch marks go, it was pretty big!" said Mom.

39

"It's not just the animal that's big," said Emily. "Look at the size of this poop!"

"It looks like we found your black bear," said Dad.

Mom asked, "Let's see what you learned today. What can you figure out about this bear?"

"It's been eating plants," said Emily, "because there's no hair or bones in this poop."

"Good job!" Mom said. "What else?"

the STRAIGHT POOP

Black bears eat almost anything. They mostly dine on leaves, nuts, berries, insects, twigs, and honey, but they also hunt small animals and fish.

"It must be as tall as you, Dad, and it has really long claws," said Michael.

"Here's its footprint," said Michael. "It's really big, and it has five toes like a raccoon instead of four like a mountain lion."

"I told you you'd be able to count a black bear's toes," laughed Dad.

"It rubbed off some black hair on the tree," said Emily. "That must be why they call them black bears!"

"All of the black bears in Olympic National Park are black," explained Mom. "But in other areas, black bears can be all different colors. They can be black, brown, or cinnamon-colored. Some black bears are almost white!"

43

As the family ate dinner that night, everyone talked about how much fun they had.

"We didn't see very many animals," said Emily, "but it seemed like we did."

Everyone laughed when Michael said, "And I didn't get scared once!"

TRACKS and

BLACK BEAR

Large tracks with five visible toes and claws.

Scat changes depending on diet but usually contains vegetation.

BLACK-TAILED MULE DEER

Each pointy hoofprint is split into two parts. Dew claws sometimes show behind each track.

Scat is oval-shaped like jellybeans. Can be in lumpy piles or even look like "cow pies."

COYOTE

Tracks are like a dog's, with four toes, usually with visible claw marks.

Scat is very dark colored with tapered ends and usually contains hair or bits of bone.

DOUGLAS SQUIRREL

Four toes on front track and five on back.

Scat is small and shapeless.

LITTLE BROWN BAT

Tracks are rarely seen because bats hardly ever land on soft ground.

Scat is runny and white.

SCAT NOTES

OLYMPIC SHORT-TAILED WEASEL

Tiny five-toed tracks (little toe often doesn't show), usually following a windy path.

Rope-like cords of scat are often found on raised objects, like rocks or stumps.

MOUNTAIN LION

Tracks are bigger than a coyote's, but claws don't show.

Scat is rarely seen because mountain lions bury it.

RACCOON

Scat and tracks large for the animal's size. Five bulbous toes.

Scat is blunt on ends, and may contain dangerous parasites.

DON'T TOUCH RACCOON SCAT!

ROOSEVELT ELK

Tracks are longer and more blunt than deer tracks. Each hoofprint is split into two parts.

Elk scat is oval-shaped like jellybeans and is quite a bit bigger than deer scat. Can be in lumpy piles or even look like "cow pies."

SPOTTED OWL

Tracks show four toes: two pointing forward and two backward or sideways.

Scat is runny and white. "Cough pellets" contain fur and bones.

ABOUT the AUTHOR and ILLUSTRATOR

GARY ROBSON lives on a ranch near Yellowstone National Park in Montana and owns a bookstore in Red Lodge. He received his teaching credential in 1987 and has taught in California and Montana colleges. He is an expert in closed captioning technology for deaf and hard-of-hearing people. Gary has written five other non-fiction books.
www.whopooped.com

ROBERT RATH is a book designer and illustrator living in Bozeman, Montana. Although he has worked with Scholastic Books, Lucasfilm, and Montana State University, his favorite project is keeping up with his family.

Who Pooped in the Park?

OTHER BOOKS IN THE WHO POOPED IN THE PARK?™ SERIES:

Acadia National Park

Glacier National Park

Grand Canyon National Park

Grand Teton National Park

Great Smoky Mountains National Park

Red Rock Canyon National Conservation Area

Rocky Mountain National Park

Sequoia and Kings Canyon National Parks

Shenandoah National Park

Sonoran Desert

Yellowstone National Park

Yosemite National Park